TRAVEL TIPS

John Townsend

Heinemann Library
Chicago, Illinois

Customer service 888-454-2279
Visit our website at www.heinemannraintree.com

Edited by Pollyanna Poulter
Designed by Philippa Jenkins and Hart MacLeod
Illustrated by Clare Elsom
Picture research by Elizabeth Alexander and Maria Joannou
Production by Alison Parsons
Originated by Modern Age Repro House Ltd.
Printed and bound in China by South China Printing Company Ltd.

13 12 11 10 09
10 9 8 7 6 5 4 3 2 1

Library of Congress Cataloging-in-Publication Data
Townsend, John, 1955-
 Travel tips / John Townsend.
     p. cm. -- (Life skills)
 Includes bibliographical references and index.
 ISBN 978-1-4329-1356-4 (hc)
 1. Travel--Juvenile literature. I. Title.
 G175.T69 2008
 910.4--dc22
                              2008005968

Acknowledgments
The Publishers would like to thank the following for permission to reproduce photographs: © Alamy Images: pp. **5** (David Noble Photography), **13** (ImageState), **33** (JLImages), **45** (Charles Ridgway), **46** (Terry Sohl); © Corbis: pp. **7**, **25** (Moodboard), **29** (Jose Fuste Raga), **37** (Tom Bean); © Getty Images: pp. **18** (Taxi/Carlos Spottorno), **43** (Photographer's Choice/ Fredrik Skold), **49** (AFP Photo/Eric Cabanis); © Lonely Planet Images: p. **38** (Andrew Marshall & Leanne Walker); © Masterfile: p. **31** (Noel Hendrickson); © Photolibrary: pp. **8** (Christie & Cole), **21** (Duncan McDougall); © Public Health Image Library: p. **35** (James Gathany); © Rex Features: pp. **15** (Sipa Press), **17**; © Science Photo Library: p. **11** (BSIP, LA); © Still Pictures: pp. **23** (Vélez/Andia), **27** (Nigel Dickinson).

Cover photograph of tourist taking picture reproduced with permission of © Istockphoto (Sharon Dominick).

The Publishers would like to thank Helena Smith for her invaluable help in the preparation of this book.

Contents

Some words are printed in bold, **like this**. You can find out what they mean by looking in the glossary.

On The Move

Right now, millions of people are on the move, traveling around the planet. People today travel more than ever before. Whether for business or pleasure, we travel farther in a year than most of our ancestors traveled in a lifetime. Technology and cheap fares mean many of us are able to travel to other countries quickly and easily. Never before has travel been such big business.

DID YOU KNOW?

The average person spends one hour and six minutes traveling every day. In a year, each person travels an average of 7,400 miles (12,000 km). Everyone on the planet combined travels nearly 17 trillion miles (25 trillion km) in a year. Of all this traveling:

- 53 percent is by car;
- 26 percent is by bus;
- 9 percent is by rail;
- 9 percent is by high-speed transportation, such as planes;
- 3 percent is by bicycle, boat, and other means.

A LONG HAUL

People take approximately 800 million trips to foreign countries each year, a number that is expected to double by 2020. Where do all these international travelers go? Most go to France. After that, Spain and the United States are top choices, followed by China and Italy.

The most popular destinations for young travelers are Australia, the United States, and France. Backpackers often head for Thailand, Australia, and New Zealand. Three out of four young travelers go overseas to explore, learn a foreign language, do volunteer work, or study. Four out of five say they return more tolerant of other cultures as a result of their travels.

"The world is a book and those who do not travel read only a page."
Saint Augustine, philosopher

By 2020, 378 million **long-haul** travelers will be on the move each year, many of them young people. Whether visiting new places with school, college, family, or friends, young travelers can learn about the world through real, unforgettable experiences.

One day you, too, may join friends on an extended trip and set off to explore new areas. Wherever you plan to go, you want to get the most from life's journeys, no matter where they take you. That's where this book can help!

| The world's top tourist destinations, 2006 ||
Country	Millions of visitors
1. France	79.1
2. Spain	58.5
3. United States	51.1
4. China	49.6
5. Italy	41.1
6. United Kingdom	30.7
7. Germany	23.6
8. Mexico	21.4
9. Austria	20.3
10. Russia	20.2

Even if you haven't been to another country, it's still likely that you'll take at least a few trips abroad in your lifetime.

Planning Your Trip

So you've saved up and it's almost time to take off. Before you walk out the door and wave good-bye, there are a few things to make sure of—wherever you're going. After all, minutes spent planning can save hours of misery while you're away.

LOOK AHEAD

Of the billions of trips every year, the majority go as planned and travelers return home looking forward to their next journey. But vacations or traveling can go very wrong for many different reasons. Poor planning before even taking off is one of those reasons. It always pays to plan ahead.

> "No one realizes how beautiful it is to travel until he comes home and rests his head on his old, familiar pillow."
>
> Lin Yutang, Chinese writer

Do your research

It's always a good idea to find out some key facts about a destination. Aside from providing ideas of extra places to go, research might suggest times to avoid. After all, it's not a good idea to arrive somewhere in the middle of a **hurricane**, transportation strike, epidemic, political unrest, or traffic gridlock. Research is also a good way to excite the travel mood.

Getting it Right

Before you start planning, ask:

- **Where?** City or countryside? Hot or cold? Coast or inland? Culture or adventure? Many people head to the same places. For example, many people in the United States head for Mexico, Canada, California, or Florida.

- **When?** When is the best time to travel? It pays to consider weather, seasons, transportation timetables, and when attractions open or close for the season.

- **Why?** Looking for an adventure? Visiting friends or family? On a school-exchange program? There are many good reasons for traveling. Knowing what yours are will help you enjoy your trip even more!

A few searches on the Internet might reveal all types of interesting information that could improve a visit. You could also go to your local library and browse the travel section for any useful books.

Be prepared

Young people who aren't used to traveling can sometimes feel **homesick** when they're away. But young people aren't the only ones who miss family, friends, pets, and familiar things. It's quite normal for all people to miss home. Some people may only feel slight loneliness, sadness, or anxiety. Others may develop stomachaches or headaches. Usually when the new surroundings become more familiar, feelings of homesickness go away.

To deal with homesickness:

- Pack photos, letters, or a favorite object to keep a small piece of home nearby.

- Talk to others. A problem shared is often a problem halved.

- Write feelings down on paper if there is no one to talk to.

- Keep in touch with people at home by texting or sending an e-mail (just remember to include such costs in your travel budget).

WHAT TO PACK

"Just in case" can be bad advice when packing for a trip! Most people are tempted to cram everything in "just in case." What to pack and what to leave behind is worth thinking about long before it's time to depart.

Some people leave packing to the last minute and don't think about the essential things they will need. Other travelers start making long lists of what to pack months before they go.

The number-one rule when packing is "if in doubt, leave it out." Moving heavy bags on and off trains, buses, and crowded stairways can be bad news—for everyone. Besides, the more you take, the more there is to lose.

Whenever possible, stick to one bag only. When hiking, just one backpack is the limit. Always remember, even suitcases with wheels can be awkward to move through busy streets or rough countryside, especially in bad weather.

Although people have different requirements, there are some basic things everyone needs on their travels. Depending on the destination, many items can be bought cheaply in most supermarkets around the world, so it's not a big deal if they get left behind.

> "When preparing to travel, lay out all your clothes and all your money. Then take half the clothes and twice the money."
>
> Susan Heller,
> U.S. writer

Trying to pack too much is a common problem!

• CHECKLIST •

- Everyday bag: to keep the items handy that you use often (tickets, camera, reading material).
- First aid kit: compact travel health kit, small nail scissors, and tweezers.
- Toiletries (in a waterproof bag): toothpaste; toothbrush; hairbrush or comb; shampoo; soap; small towel; deodorant, etc.
- Mobile phone and charger (and adapter if you are going abroad).
- Money carrier and small padlock. Use a money belt or neck wallet to keep money (and passport when abroad) secure.

- Travel watch or alarm.
- Flashlight or head lamp.
- Sunglasses and sunscreen: protect your eyes and skin from harmful rays, especially if traveling at higher altitudes, in bright sunlight, or in snow.
- Travel organizer: for carrying identification, tickets, addresses, and phone numbers.
- Positive attitude! Travel sometimes means dealing with the unexpected, so it always helps to take along a big smile.

Getting it Right

Cramming the most stuff into a small bag is a skill. Remember to put the items that will be needed first on arrival at the top. Plenty of plastic bags are helpful, too. Some travelers prefer to roll up clothes for packing, to reduce creases. Small, soft items, such as socks, are good for packing around hard edges or anything breakable. Remember to pack small items inside shoes to save space, and don't forget to label luggage clearly.

GOING ABROAD

It was once rare for young people to visit other countries. Today, international travel is common for millions of young travelers. The first time abroad can be both exciting and daunting, especially if the traveler doesn't speak the language. This is why it pays to learn as much as you can about a country and its customs, rules, and **etiquette** before you travel to it.

How passports work

A passport is an internationally recognized travel document that proves the identity and nationality of the traveler. A current passport is required to enter and leave most countries.

A **visa** is a special document that may be required to enter another country, especially for travelers who plan to work in that country or stay for a long period. A visa must be obtained from the **embassy** of the country you are visiting. Details and advice can be obtained from the various passport offices.

In some countries, you must carry your passport at all times. If not, it's always best to leave the passport somewhere safe, making sure there's a photocopy somewhere else. If the passport gets lost or stolen, the copy should help the nearest embassy get a replacement within a few days.

• CHECKLIST •

- Passport (up to date) with a copy of its number kept separately.
- A simple phrasebook and dictionary.
- Money (in the correct currency) and travel insurance.
- List of emergency addresses and telephone numbers—in your mobile phone, and written down, in case it's lost or stolen.
- Telephone number of your embassy.
- Phone charger and adapter (for different power sockets).

Getting it Right

When entering and leaving countries, it is necessary to go through customs, where travelers and their luggage may be searched. Make sure you are not carrying anything forbidden or anyone else's luggage.

Other preparations

Before traveling to other countries, first find out which **vaccinations** are required. The World Health Organization provides up-to-date information on which inoculations are needed for different countries. It clearly states: "It is the traveler's responsibility to ask for information, to understand the risks involved, and to take the necessary precautions for the journey."

Foreign money is often confusing, so it's well worth doing some homework to find out the exact **exchange rate**. A good online currency converter can show the value of most world currencies. It's just a matter of typing in an amount of money and clicking a button to get its value in another currency. Easy!

People in different countries do not all set their clocks and watches to show the same time as yours. Instead, people live in different time zones. Check what time zone you are traveling to, and be prepared to change your watch to the local time.

For security, take some money in the form of traveler's checks. Or keep your money in an account at home and use ATMs to withdraw it.

Visit your doctor at least a month in advance of your trip, to find out which inoculations you will need.

11

GETTING THERE

You've done your research, packed your bags, and you're ready to go—but the big question facing every traveler is, "How?" What type of transportation is best? The answer to that question depends on where you want to go.

MANY ROADS TO CROSS

Wherever you plan to travel, whether close to home or far away, you're actually more likely to use roads than anything else. In fact, 80 percent of all travel is by road. While there are more roads in the United States than anywhere else, Europe's roads are far busier.

Bicycle

Many young people get their first taste of independent travel from setting off by bike to explore areas close to home before venturing further. Some adventurous travelers put their bike on a bus or train then explore a new area by pedal power on the open road. Bicycle rentals or **tandem** rentals with a friend (it has to be a *good* friend!) is a great way to see new places.

TIP

For long bicycle trips:

- Relax as you ride, and take a break every hour.

- Eat frequently, in small amounts.

- Stay well hydrated.

- Avoid numb hands by wearing cycling gloves.

- Take talcum powder to avoid and treat chafing.

- Plan for all weather (for details about checking weather conditions, see page 52).

DID YOU KNOW?

The world's worst traffic jam happened in France in the summer of 2001. The line stretched 410 miles (660 km), from Paris to Toulouse.

Car travel

Most families tend to travel by car for at least part of their vacation. Cramming in luggage, the dog, food, and other extras can be a nightmare! A long journey can seem even longer if the travelers feel bored, sick, or both!

You can prevent carsickness by being prepared. Always bring games or activities to do if you go on a long car trip. Sitting in the front of the car, or having a clear view of the road, also helps. Singing along to music, or playing games that encourage looking ahead, can prevent problems. And make sure the car is well ventilated.

Buses

One of the best ways for young people to travel cheaply is by bus, so it's always worth considering the services available. (See page 52 for more information on national bus services.)

Getting it Right

Moving from one place to another has always carried risks. Roads can be dangerous—especially in unfamiliar places. Whether you plan to cycle or just walk, you need to be aware of the "rules of the road" wherever you happen to be. An important rule for young people traveling by road is never hitchhike, not even in a group.

When traveling around the United States, Canada, or Australia, the famous Greyhound buses have routes to and from thousands of places.

13

BOATS AND TRAINS

Sea travel has always held great excitement, mystery, and adventure. Sadly, it can also hold storms, icebergs, and seasickness! Even so, going on cruise ships has never been more popular. Cruises designed especially for young people are more and more common.

With some cruises, travelers can leave the ship at any port along their journey. Without all the extras of large, expensive cruises, some options allow student travelers to get across the seas much more cheaply. But remember: the smaller the ship, the greater the chance of feeling seasick.

Rail travel

If sailing the oceans doesn't appeal, how about a glamorous train trip across Russia and China along the famous Silk Route? The Trans-Siberian Express and China Orient Express are among the world's most **prestigious** trains.

Traveling by train can be a great way to get around and see the world through a window, often with the most spectacular scenery. Some young people may dismiss rail travel as being too expensive, but it doesn't have to be.

Getting it Right

To ease seasickness:

- Get as much fresh air as possible away from the smell of fuel fumes and food. Go out on deck and focus on the horizon or something that isn't moving—don't watch the waves!

- Inside, find a seat in the middle of the ship on a lower deck. This is where the ship moves least.

- Avoid heavy meals before traveling.

- Lie still with your eyes shut.

- Anti-sickness medicines should be taken before travel, and according to the directions, so they have time to be absorbed by the body.

- Ginger snaps help some people, or ginger-flavored tea. Also pack some peppermint-flavored candies or tea, since both can help with seasickness.

- **Acupressure** can be applied with a wristband or by pressing a finger against the middle of the wrist.

Look out for special deals or passes for young travelers, and keep in mind some of the positive points of rail travel.

- Trains allow travelers to move easily between cities. Most train stations are near tourist centers and have hotels nearby.

- Sleeping on sleeper trains saves time and some of the cost of a hotel.

- Moving effortlessly between destinations on a train, travelers can talk to local passengers, get travel information from other travelers, read a good book, or just sit back and enjoy the view!

- It's a greener way to travel than by bus or plane.

Maybe not all trains let you relax—you might not always get a seat!

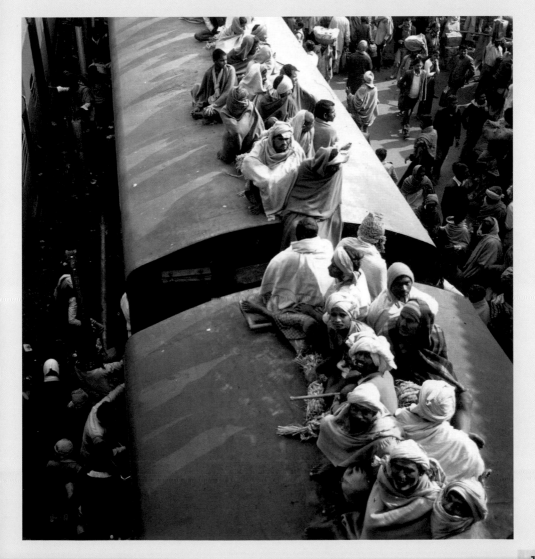

UP AND AWAY

The average number of travelers flying over the United States in any hour is roughly 61,000 people. That equals millions of air passengers per year! Of them, approximately 5 million are people younger than 18, traveling alone. In fact, air travel for young people is big business, and they are well taken care of by many airlines!

Check before flying

The rules about how much luggage you can take on planes are always changing, so it's important to check with the airline before you pack. What is banned to carry in hand luggage can also change from airport to airport and from country to country, so it pays to check in advance to avoid having substances confiscated. Also, don't forget that luggage can get lost, so never pack valuables!

When you are ready to go to the airport, always leave with plenty of time to spare. Check traffic reports for any likely delays. Many people fail to give themselves enough time to get to the airport. Minimum check-in times vary. The latest cut-off is usually 30 minutes before the departure time, but for long-haul flights check-in is often much earlier.

When checking in for your flight, be sure to confirm any special requests, such as meal specifications, that you made when booking your flight. If you suffer from airsickness, ask for a seat over the wing, where the plane is most stable. Tilt your seat back, rest your head on the headrest, and close your eyes.

Listening to music helps some people relax and can take their mind off feeling sick or scared of flying. However, you must turn off electrical equipment during take-off and landing, since the equipment can interfere with the aircraft's computer signals.

Bad weather or mechanical problems can ruin the best plans—but you should get there eventually!

When things go wrong

In an ideal world, airlines would never have delays, no flights would be canceled, and the weather would be great. But in the real world, even with the best-laid plans, weather can turn bad and connections can be missed. When flights don't run as planned, always stay calm and be patient.

If your flight is canceled, remain at the gate with other passengers and listen for instructions. There may be free meal certificates or hotel vouchers being given out. Ask at your airline's desk about rebooking a flight that has been canceled.

Getting it Right

- Never try to hide anything at the airport.
- Keep your flight number handy, as well as the departure time and the terminal from which you are departing.
- Keep a good book handy in case of delays at the airport.

During the flight

Pay close attention to the safety talk at the beginning of the flight so you know where to find your nearest exit and what to do in case of an emergency. Drink juice or water to make sure you stay hydrated. Try doing seated leg exercises to help prevent stiffness.

On arrival

When you arrive at your destination, report any problems (such as damaged or lost baggage) to the airline before leaving the airport. If damage was impossible to notice until much later, call the airline as soon as possible to find out what to do.

Getting it Wrong

- Never joke about hijackings or bombings. It is against the law.
- Never accept packages or letters from strangers, and never carry anything onto a plane for anyone else.
- Never leave your luggage unattended.

⬇ *Despite some people being worried about flying, it can be relaxing and is one of the safest ways to travel.*

GETTING THERE

1) When planning to travel, what is most important?
a) Going to a quiet place far from other people.
b) Getting a real bargain with lots of cheap attractions.
c) Finding a tourist center that's exciting with lots to do and plenty to buy.

2) When packing your bags, what do you take?
a) As few clothes as possible, since personal hygiene doesn't matter when you're away.
b) As much as you can so you don't have to buy anything when you're away.
c) All your best clothes so you're ready to party.

3) When planning a trip, do you:
a) get a book from the library about remote wilderness vacations?
b) search the Internet for cheap fares and budget accommodations?
c) ask a travel agent to do it all for you and let them choose?

4) To get to your destination, do you:
a) pay a bit extra to make sure you don't have to sit with young children and tourists?
b) get the cheapest ticket even if it means sleeping at the station between connections?
c) choose the fastest and most exciting way to travel?

5) What is your idea of a perfect meal when traveling?
a) A delicious meal you've cooked for yourself on a campfire under the stars.
b) Getting invited to someone's home to sample the local cooking and company.
c) A candle-lit dinner with lots of people and piles of food cooked by an award-winning chef.

6) Who do you like to be with on your travels most of all?
a) Yourself.
b) Local people who treat you as their guest.
c) Friends you make when traveling.

See page 50 to find out what type of traveler you are!

WHERE TO STAY

Think about where you want to stay before you try to find accommodations. Some people insist on comfort, style, and luxury while others just want a bed for the night for the lowest price possible. The more you pay, the better the service is likely to be—although that isn't always the case. Horror stories are sometimes told of cockroaches and mice scurrying in expensive accommodations, while some of the cheapest hotels can offer excellent service.

GRADING PLACES

Travel guides and Internet searches are the best way to find out about accommodations. In many countries, hotels are graded with a star system. The more stars the hotel has by its name (five is usually the maximum, but not always), the more services it provides. However, there is no international agreement as to what the number of stars actually means. It is up to the traveler to check each hotel's list of facilities.

If you do not book accommodations in advance, always look at a room before you take it. It is the traveler's right to look at a room before committing to stay in it.

(See pages 52 and 53 for details of some useful websites and guides that can assist you with planning your stay.)

Getting it Right

It is advisable to book accommodations well in advance, especially at busy times of the year. When making a reservation by telephone or online, keep a record of the confirmation number, the name of the person who took the reservation, and the quoted rate. Remember that the hotel's rate, or price, is likely to be higher at the busiest times.

It always pays to check the accommodation before booking, just in case you don't like a highway under your window, bedbugs, dirty bathrooms, bad food, a damp mattress, or dripping ceilings!

TYPES OF ACCOMMODATIONS

Hotel

A place where guests pay to stay for a short time, sometimes with services such as a restaurant, swimming pool, or meeting rooms. Modern hotels usually have many bedrooms, often with air-conditioning and room service. In Australia, though, a hotel might mean just a bar.

Guesthouse

Often the name given to a small hotel, offering just a few rooms and limited services to paying guests.

Self-catering accommodation

Where rooms are available to rent. Rooms include a kitchen for travelers to prepare their own meals.

B & B (Bed and Breakfast)

Often a family-run home or farmhouse with a few bedrooms available. Paying guests are given a room to sleep in at night and breakfast the following morning. Guests are expected to leave the premises after breakfast.

Motel

A hotel for motorists. Motels usually have good access to the road network or are purpose-built, out of town, on a major route.

Hostel

Popular with young travelers. Guests can rent a bed, often located in a communal or shared sleeping space. Bathroom, kitchen, and lounge areas are also shared. (See page 22 for more information on hostels.)

YOUTH HOSTELS

An organization exists for young people on the move that need cheap, reliable accommodations for just a night or two. Today, by joining the Youth Hostel Association (**YHA**), anyone can stay cheaply in one of the thousands of YHA hostels around the world. They provide accommodations where guests can rent a bed (sometimes a bunk bed in a **dormitory**) and share a bathroom, kitchen, and lounge or games room.

One of the great things about staying in a hostel is that you can meet a variety of people, often from many countries. Hostels are places where travelers can share experiences, get to understand other cultures, and make good friends.

How it started out

Richard Schirrmann was a German schoolteacher. He wanted to enrich the lives of young people living in large cities by letting them enjoy the countryside. He opened the world's first Youth Hostel in Germany in 1909. The Youth Hostels Association of Great Britain was later formed to combine hiking, cycling, and youth organizations. It provided simple accommodations for walkers and cyclists traveling throughout the United Kingdom.

Finding a hostel

The YHA has 4,000 hostels all around the world in more than 80 countries, under the name Hostelling International (HI). It boasts: "Unlike bland motels, impersonal hotels or dodgy backpacker houses, HI youth hostels are fun, lively meeting places, full of like-minded people." In order to stay at a YHA hostel, be sure to take your YHA membership card with you.

Each year, millions of young people visit the United States from around the world. Hostelling International USA provides travelers with information, a comfortable stay, and access to cheap travel.

The downside of hostel accommodation for some travelers is the lack of privacy. Sharing a dormitory is very different than staying in a private hotel room. There can be noises from people snoring, returning late, or leaving early. That's why many youth hostels fix times for last admissions and lights out.

DID YOU KNOW?

Hostels were once run with very strict rules, where all visitors had to perform cleaning duties and other tasks. Today, they are far more informal. Older people can use hostels, too—so long as they are young at heart!

Getting it Right

Staying in a hostel can be a good choice because:

- They are low in price compared to hotels and B&Bs.
- Communal areas mean guests mix more than in hotels.
- Most hostels have a good community feel and are far more relaxed than hotels. This gives guests the chance to make new friends and share stories and travel tips.
- Most hostels have a library of travel guides for guests to use to plan their journey.
- Hostel staff are usually friendly and willing to help, providing free advice on local places to check out.

A youth hostel common room is a great place to meet other young travelers.

CAMPING

Walking through the countryside with a backpack is good exercise and a great way to explore nature. There's nothing quite like walking in the great outdoors, pitching a tent, and sleeping under the stars!

Many hikers prefer to use official campsites with all types of facilities available. Campsites usually cost just a small amount and provide a safe, clean environment. As for the hiking, the only real cost involved is the equipment needed. With a group of people, a lot can be shared.

Benefits of hiking

- It gives you a chance to get away and forget about the everyday stresses of life.
- It's a way of relaxing but also a chance to test skills and abilities.
- In a hiking party, it's easy to share the various jobs and responsibilities with a group of friends.

It's always better for young or inexperienced hikers to travel in a group. That way, if someone gets hurt or sick, there are others to help. A group of at least three is safest. A lot can be learned from fellow hikers who know more about camping. The best way to learn the basics of camping and to develop skills is to travel with more experienced hikers.

Camping is a healthy way for a group of friends to see new places and enjoy traveling cheaply.

• CHECKLIST •

- Hiking boots and backpack.
- Tent, poles, hammer, tarp, sleeping bag, mattress, pillow, blankets, air pump, rope, stakes.
- All-weather clothing (i.e. rain gear).
- Map, compass, flashlight and batteries, lantern, drinking water, radio, canteen, clock, camera, tent repair gear, pocket knife, lighter, tissues, water-purification tablets.
- First aid kit with tweezers to remove splinters.
- Kitchen utensils: food container, pans, stove, fuel, matches/ lighter, paper plates, bowls, mugs, thermos, aluminum foil, towel, tongs, bottle/can opener, knife, dish soap, sponge, garbage bags.

Getting it Right

If staying at a campsite, check the rules and facilities, since there may be many regulations. If camping "in the wild":

- Make sure you are staying in a place that is not off-limits.

- Find a spot that is safe and protected. Camp away from hilltops, where there's no protection from strong winds and lightning. Avoid the very lowest ground since it might flood in heavy rain.

- Find natural obstacles that provide windbreaks and shelter. Trees and rocks are good natural barriers. Don't pitch a tent right under a tree in case of lightning or falling branches.

- If possible, camp near a stream, river, or lake so there's water for washing and cleaning up. Don't get too close though, in case there are flash floods.

BRIGHT LIGHTS, BIG CITY

Are you dazzled by the bright lights of big cities? Many of us are attracted far more by the hustle and bustle of cities than by camping in the peaceful outdoors. So what do you need to know before visiting a large city that you've never been to before?

CAPITAL COSTS

The first thing to keep in mind in the biggest cities of the world is that you often have to pay the biggest prices. The cost of food, entertainment, transportation, attractions, and shopping—some of the very reasons many of us like to visit city centers—can be far higher than anywhere else. Although sightseeing in busy, capital cities usually has great appeal, be prepared for high prices.

Wherever you are in the world, visit local markets and try haggling with the vendors. Fruit, jewelry, clothes, souvenirs ... you name it—you're bound to find some bargains.

TIP

The world's 10 most expensive cities	
City	**Country**
1. Moscow	Russia
2. London	Great Britain
3. Seoul	South Korea
4. Tokyo	Japan
5. Hong Kong	China
6. Copenhagen	Denmark
7. Geneva	Switzerland
8. Osaka	Japan
9. Zurich	Switzerland
10. Oslo	Norway

Mercer's 2007 survey. http://money.cnn com/2007/06/15/pf/most_expensive_cities

According to the cost of transportation, food, clothing, housing, household goods, and entertainment, the most expensive city to visit is Moscow, followed by London. Among North American cities, New York and Los Angeles are the most expensive and the only two to rank in the top 50 of the world's most expensive cities.

Despite the fact that London is the second most expensive city in the world, more than 15 million travelers from overseas visit Britain's capital every year. Many of them are young students on trips with schools and colleges.

Top 10 city destinations 2006		
City	**Ranking**	**Millions of foreign tourist arrivals**
London	1	15.64
Bangkok	2	10.35
Paris	3	9.70
Singapore	4	9.50
Hong Kong	5	8.14
New York City	6	6.22
Dubai	7	6.12
Rome	8	6.03
Seoul	9	4.92
Barcelona	10	4.70

Source: http://www.euromonitor.com/Top_150_City_Destinations_London_Leads_the_Way

Must-see

New York is the top, must-see city in the United States. About 40 million foreign and U.S. tourists visit each year. Among New York's main attractions are the Empire State Building, Ellis Island, Broadway theater shows, world-class museums, the Bronx Zoo, and the New York Botanical Garden. After all that sightseeing, any traveler is likely to be hungry. Here, the choice of places to eat is like nowhere else in the world.

PLANNING AHEAD

When heading for a new city, the temptation is to forget about the homework. After all, cities have everything, so why not wait to get there before worrying about accommodations and places to see? But planning in advance saves travelers a lot of time and expense.

With just a few brochures, guidebooks, a good street map, and Internet searches, city travelers are ready to take on the entire city experience. Knowing such information in advance helps give a stranger to a city a mental map and idea of where places worth visiting are found in relation to each other.

DID YOU KNOW?

The World Youth & Student Educational Travel Confederation conducted a worldwide survey of young travelers. The survey shows that 80 percent of young travelers use the Internet to search for travel information before departing, with 50 percent booking transportation and accommodations online.

Getting it Right

Some countries, especially in the Middle East and Asia, dress more conservatively than many Western countries. You shouldn't wear shorts or sleeveless tops in these places. Some holy places, such as St. Peter's Cathedral in Rome, Italy, require you to cover your arms when entering the building. You don't want to miss out on seeing such great places just because you don't meet the dress code!

Be streetwise

Wherever you're traveling to, get some local knowledge. Read up on local laws and customs to avoid offending people or breaking local laws without realizing it.

Knowing the local rules of the road can keep visitors from being fined or even arrested. For example, just crossing the street in some cities is a **jaywalking** offense, if a proper pedestrian crossing isn't used. Even accidentally dropping a ticket or brochure could be a litter offense, with an instant fine being charged.

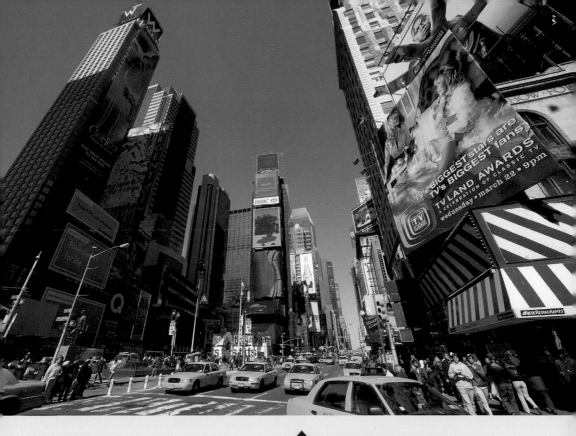

Always be aware of belongings and valuables. Be careful when out on crowded streets. Pickpockets are always on the lookout for confused tourists. Be prepared for the worst and leave copies of ticket numbers, your passport, insurance, and contact details somewhere safe—just in case.

Finally, stay with friends, don't wander off alone, and keep your mobile phone handy. Always leave details of your travel plans with someone else, such as family or friends back home. (See page 42 for more on travel and crime.)

Whatever a tourist might wish for, it can probably be found in New York. Maybe that's why so many young people continue to be attracted by the hustle and bustle of this great city.

TIP

Make a list of what to see, with a timetable of when to go, having researched transportation routes and open days.

City travel

Walking around a city might look straightforward on a map and appear easy when first setting off. However, in bad weather, or after a long day of sightseeing, even the hardiest visitor is likely to need another mode of transportation. Many cities have excellent transportation services around the centers, but the cost soon adds up. By checking costs in advance, the city traveler can get some good deals on bus, subway, and train tickets. A daily pass is often much cheaper than buying tickets for every trip, especially if you plan on making several trips.

In some of the larger world capitals, a public transportation service (such as the subway) is a quick way to get around. Get a pocket map of the public transit system in advance, although most stations will have small route maps available. Be warned: maps aren't always to scale. Although stations on the map may look like they're right next to each other, it probably isn't really the case!

Use common sense when traveling around a city after dark. Stick to main streets, particularly in unfamiliar areas. If you're not sure about a destination or the safety of an area, take a taxi. If you do take the subway or an underground train late at night, ride in cars with more people inside.

DID YOU KNOW?

A British woman recently designed two rings, to be worn on a finger of each hand, that keep the wearer from getting lost. With a small control device worn around the neck that displays numbers, the wearer just types in the address of a place to find. An electronic compass and GPS system sends signals to the two rings. Small vibrating motors make the rings buzz to tell the wearer to turn left or right, go forward or backward. Both rings buzz at once if the person goes in the wrong direction. Maybe we'll all be wearing them soon!

Getting lost

Even with a map, it's very easy to get lost in some of the bigger cities of the world. Imagine emerging from a Tokyo subway into a huge bustling street and trying to find street signs, without knowing any Japanese. That's why more city travelers are using personal satellite navigation devices (SAT-NAVs) to help them get around. This technology is often called a GPS (Global Positioning Satellite) system.

GPSs can be used in any city in the world. They tell you exactly where you are and how to get to where you want to go.

In the middle of a city, help isn't far away. Just ask for the nearest:

- Tourist information center;
- Hospital;
- Embassy (if abroad);
- Police station;
- Reception staff (in a hotel).

HEALTH AND SAFETY

Some people feel that travel is riskier to their health than everyday life. Truthfully, though, the most dangerous part of a trip is the car ride to the airport! In fact, the risk of an inactive lifestyle is greater than travel accidents, natural disasters, and shark attacks combined.

HARD TO SWALLOW

The majority of travelers have a great and healthy time away. However, there are still precautions every traveler should take before leaving in order to help avoid the more common health problems.

Food and drink

One of the delights of traveling to different areas is sampling regional dishes, foreign cooking, and unusual food. However, a common problem that tourists face is turista, or diarrhea. One of the reasons travelers are prone to illness is that their **immune system** isn't always used to some of the **micro-organisms** found in unfamiliar places. Therefore, it's even more important than normal to wash hands frequently with soap and hot water when traveling to different places.

DID YOU KNOW?

A real fear of traveling is called hodophobia. And it isn't always a fear of flying. A fear of trains or of traveling in cars can also be part of this phobia. Some sufferers are afraid of strange places, open places, or of contact with strangers.

Bottle it!

One of the warnings often given to travelers going abroad is to only drink bottled water. This is because of the risk from "foreign" water organisms. The same goes for campers, since even the cleanest looking stream could be contaminated. With a little extra care, and basic medication in the first aid kit just in case, there's no reason why even the most adventurous traveler has to spend the entire trip in the bathroom!

- When you are in a place without proper **sanitation**, don't brush your teeth with tap water. Also, be careful about ice cubes in drinks, and close your mouth in the shower!

- When camping, the rule is: "boil it, cook it, peel it, or forget it!" Thorough cooking is always important.

- With meat, be extra careful and make sure it's well done on the inside. Remember, the more the food is cooked, the more likely it is that harmful bacteria have been killed.

- Do not put your fingers in your mouth, and touch food as little as possible with your hands.

- Be careful when eating that thirst-quenching melon. Bacteria can live inside melons, too, so it's better to avoid them.

- Rice contains many types of bacteria. The bacteria multiply as the rice cools. Only eat freshly cooked, hot rice.

- Take great care with shellfish—another common cause of travelers' food poisoning. But, good news, hot pizza is safe! The high heat of a pizza oven tends to kill any harmful bacteria.

Some of the food for sale on your travels might be unfamiliar!

Be prepared

Being sick far away from home or in another country is an unpleasant experience. But it is one that can be avoided. The usual illnesses most travelers get are not serious, but they can cause problems if medical help is far away or if you don't speak the local language. It's therefore useful to have something handy in a first aid kit to relieve headaches, diarrhea, and insect bites when traveling abroad.

It is also necessary, of course, to take any medical supplies used on a regular basis, since they may be hard to find in another country. That includes any prescription drugs, such as inhalers and **allergy** medication. It's a good idea to pack some over-the-counter allergy medication just in case. Travelers can sometimes develop allergic reactions to all types of things in a new environment.

Getting it Right

For trips to the tropics, add **anti-malarial** tablets and water purification tablets to your first aid kit. After all, there could be deadly creatures in both the air and water—and they're often unseen.

• CHECKLIST •

Just in case you need to seek medical help abroad, it's wise to carry a short medical history list, with the following information on it:

- name, address, home telephone number as well as a parent's daytime telephone number,

- blood type,

- vaccinations you've had,

- doctor's name, address, and office and emergency telephone numbers,

- the name, address, telephone number, and details of any health or travel insurance,

- a list of any ongoing health problems and any current medications being taken,

- a list of allergies to medications, food, insects, and animals.

Use repellents and mosquito nets to keep blood-sucking insects away.

Mosquitoes

Mosquito species vary all around the world. They can be especially dangerous in the tropics where they can spread **malaria**. Mosquito bites can become very itchy and sore and can swell up if they become infected. When traveling to places where mosquitoes are common, it is important to use a mosquito repellent and to sleep under a mosquito net. Try to get a room with a large fan (the draft makes it harder for mosquitoes to fly).

Flesh wounds

Any flesh wound in the tropics is a health risk since infection can hit hard. It's good advice to carry good bandages, especially those that seal a wound against air and water, while at the same time allowing the skin to breathe. A small amount of disinfectant and antiseptic cream in the first aid kit is useful for cleaning wounds. It's then best to get any bites, scratches, and cuts checked by a doctor, just to make sure.

extremes

Being prepared for all conditions is one of the challenges facing travelers going to many regions. Stories of travelers packing warm clothing when going to cool places, only to face a heat wave, or expecting to sunbathe on a tropical beach, only to be chilled by bitterly cold winds, are all too common. Once again, a little research and being prepared can help ensure your long-awaited vacation isn't spent suffering in unsuitable clothes.

Hidden dangers

Hiking is a great way to enjoy the great outdoors, but care must always be taken. The weather can change quickly, so it's always best to be prepared for all weather. Carry extra layers for the cold and rain gear for the rain. Remember: the wind can cause **wind chill** or, in sunny conditions, even sunburn. Covering the skin is important both in cold winds and hot sun. In fact, hiking in very hot conditions can cause heat exhaustion.

Hiking should never be attempted once temperatures reach 100°F (37°C). Even the healthiest young people can experience medical problems, even death, in such extreme conditions.

DID YOU KNOW?

Extreme heat and high altitude commonly lead to health issues among tourists. Both conditions are present at one of the most popular tourist attractions in the United States. Nearly 5 million people visit the Grand Canyon National Park in Arizona each year. It is one of the natural wonders of the world. Moving sun and shadows on the rock layers produce a breathtaking display of colors. These great cliffs were carved by the Colorado River, now snaking through the bottom of the canyon. The only way down is by hiking or riding mules down steep trails. The high altitude at the top of the Grand Canyon sometimes causes visitors to experience difficulties, especially if they have breathing or heart problems. For most people walking at this altitude can be a struggle.

TIP

When hiking, always carry plenty of water, sunscreen, and a hat with a brim or peak.

Altitude sickness

At a higher altitude than you're used to, you may experience problems such as headaches, **dehydration**, and shortness of breath. Some people are affected at 5,000 feet (1,500 meters), but others aren't affected until they reach altitudes of 10,000 feet (3,000 meters) or more. Dehydration is when a person loses more fluids than they take in. If you ignore your thirst, dehydration can slow you down or even be dangerous.

Getting it **Right**

The best prevention for altitude sickness is gradually to increase your altitude every day to get used to it. It's always best to see a doctor before leaving home if you are planning to visit places at high altitudes.

Visitors to the Grand Canyon are warned not to hike from the top down to the river and back in one day because of the danger of dehydration and heat exhaustion.

Health tips for hiking in extreme conditions

- Double your calorie intake and double your fun! Salty snacks and water or sports drinks should be consumed on any hike lasting longer than 30 minutes. Food is your body's fuel.

- Do drink one quart (one liter) of water or sports drink for every hour hiking. Your best defense against sickness and exhaustion is to eat a large breakfast, a full lunch, a snack every time you take a drink, and a full meal at the end of the day. This is not a time to diet!

- Do know what your destination is.

- Do balance your food intake with fluid. With exertion, you lose salt and need to replace it or you may get sick.

- Do hike intelligently. You are responsible for your own safety as well as that of everyone in your party.

Getting it Wrong

- Never hike alone.
- Don't overestimate what you can do.

Hiking around the Grand Canyon can be hard work but the views are breath taking.

HAVING FUN

1) If going hiking, would you:
a) throw anything you can find in a backpack and hope for the best?
b) call some friends to join you and share the carrying?
c) map out your hiking route, with a detailed time plan, and label snacks for when they should be eaten?

2) If going to a new city, would you:
a) just show up and see what's going on?
b) head straight for the bright lights and entertainment?
c) make a list of places to visit, in alphabetical order, with map references and telephone numbers?

3) To make sure you don't get lost on your travels, would you:
a) trust your sense of direction or just ask the way to places?
b) rely on friends to plan your route and go with the flow?
c) take three maps, a SAT-NAV, and a compass?

4) If you were to go to another country, would you:
a) forget the phrase book and just use signs and a warm smile?
b) try out every eating place you can find, letting friends choose the first few?
c) avoid eating and drinking, and wash your hands every hour?

5) If you were to go to a sunny beach, would you:
a) slap on the sunscreen and just chill?
b) dive in and organize a surfing competition?
c) cover up, using a sunhat and umbrella, and cover yourself in insect repellent?

6) If you were to go to the Grand Canyon, would you:
a) sit on one of the mules and let it take you wherever it likes?
b) set off on a group hike and hope to go white-water rafting?
c) take extra oxygen to help you breathe and a huge water bottle to avoid dehydration?

See page 50 to find out what type of adventurer you are!

TROUBLESHOOTING

What's the worst thing that could happen on your travels? If you made a list of all the likely setbacks, you'd never want to go anywhere! Even though most trips are trouble-free, you do sometimes have to consider what to do if something goes wrong.

WORST-CASE SITUATIONS

You can't prepare for all travel nightmares, but it helps if you know some of the things to do if and when they strike. Nobody likes to think about what can go wrong while they're on vacation—since the whole point of travel is to have fun. But setbacks can, and do, happen. While you can't always avoid them, you can make plans.

Lost and don't speak the language?

Whatever happens, don't panic! There's no immediate danger. Stay calm and remember your manners. People are usually very friendly to lost strangers. Finding a police officer is the best thing to do—or head for a major tourist attraction where there should be many people to ask, including someone who speaks your language! Make sure you have a good map of the area with you at all times when you set out.

Getting it Wrong

When traveling abroad, it is important that everyone is aware of the rules, customs, and laws of the country being visited. It is no excuse to say, "I'm very sorry but I didn't know I was breaking the law." Young people, sports fans, and students are sometimes arrested for "inappropriate behavior" in public areas, such as being noisy or appearing threatening in a large group. If people get into trouble with the police while traveling abroad, they must remain calm and polite, and contact the local embassy for help.

Sick or injured?

No one should travel abroad without travel insurance, which covers the cost of medical treatment. Whether with an organized tour, family, or friends, each person's policy should cover the cost of transportation to get to a hospital, hospital fees, and getting home. All a traveler needs is the travel insurance paperwork, should an emergency arise.

A good phrasebook can be a traveler's best friend.

TIP

When you arrive at a new hotel, always write down its name and telephone number to keep in a safe pocket in case you get lost. By bringing a phrasebook, you should also be able to communicate a few well-chosen phrases if you need to, such as "help," "I'm lost," and "thank you."

CRIME

Wherever young people travel, they should always be alert for criminals at work. Thieves are often on the lookout for anyone with valuables worth stealing—such as mobile phones. Theft happens everywhere, but on vacation, when you have few possessions with you, it can be even more devastating. Although no one can stop crime, most travelers can try to keep themselves from becoming victims. They do this by being constantly aware of their surroundings, personal safety, and keeping their wits about them.

Should you become a victim of crime, it is essential to report it at once to the local police. This applies wherever you happen to be traveling at the time.

Tips to reduce the risk of being a target

- Act confidently. Avoid drawing attention by "looking like a tourist." Don't stand on street corners looking at maps, but walk confidently, since this will deter many criminals.

- Use a money belt, and don't carry all of your cash in one place. If you need to organize your wallet or check your money, go into a store to do so. In crowded subways, keep a wallet in a front pocket, rather than out of your sight. Keep purses closed and held in front or, better still, use secret pockets.

- Don't flaunt jewelry, cameras, souvenirs, or cash in public.

- Dress down so you don't look too flashy or draw attention to yourself.

- Be aware at all times and listen to your instincts. Tourists become victims when they're caught off guard, forget to keep a lookout, or wander away from others.

Getting it Wrong

Never open your hotel room door before identifying who is at the door. Never leave your hotel alone or with someone you have just met. Never give out the number of your hotel room. Never agree to meet strangers in unknown places. Avoid quiet, badly lit areas or the "scary" parts of town, and always stay with others. All travelers should always be aware of local customs, cultures, and attitudes to keep from offending, especially if visiting places of worship. All young travelers should keep with their group leaders or guardian at all times.

Stranger danger

Meeting new people is all part of the traveling experience and a great way to learn about new places. Sadly, the traveler has to be aware that not everybody is what, or whom, they seem.

When young people are on vacation, they go out mingling, partying, and meeting new people. That is when they are most vulnerable to being fooled. Travelers need to be careful of strangers and always be wary of what anybody offers, since there are a lot of scam artists around. Of course, that doesn't mean you can't trust anyone, but it's sometimes best to be suspicious of everyone at first.

Be aware that although crime is rare, it does happen.

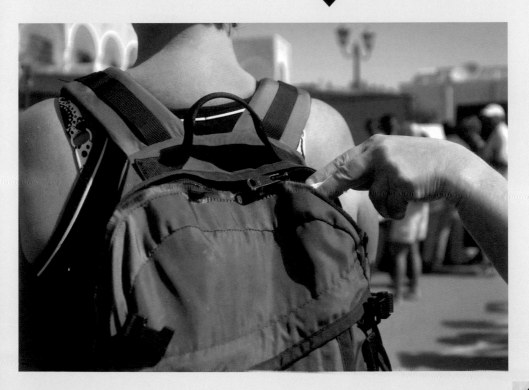

43

DANGERS AND SETBACKS

No matter where you go on your travels, if nature strikes, things can get scary. Very rarely do tourists become caught up in floods, hurricanes, earthquakes, or giant **tsunamis**. There's very little anyone can do to prepare for such events, but there are a few common-sense things to do in case of any sudden confusion and lack of services following a major incident.

The first thing to check when checking into a hotel is what its emergency procedure is. Hotels should also have some idea of disaster possibilities, emergency supplies, and a general plan. However, this all depends on the quality of the hotel.

If a disaster is serious, it's likely all phones will be out of action. There is likely to be much confusion at first. When possible, travelers abroad should contact their embassy. They will collect names of the **nationals** affected, inform families back home, and organize evacuations.

Preparing for the worst

So how can a traveler ever be prepared? After all, some of the most amazing parts of the world are prone to dangerous weather conditions from time to time.

Always find out what the weather forecast is at your destination for the week ahead. Typing a place name or zip code into a weather website

(see page 52 for details) will tell you just what conditions to expect. Even so, it's still wise to keep checking, up to the time of departure, since weather forecasts can change!

Wherever you go with your friends on vacation, or when traveling, it is important to stay with them, or close by them, at all times. Keep checking on each other. If you do get separated, try to contact each other at least every hour or so. Also, arrange a meeting place in advance in case you get split up.

Despite the passing danger of a tornado in 2007, Disney World, with its thousands of visitors, remained safe.

SCARY ANIMALS

Local animal populations can be dangerous, especially if you are camping out in the wild. Two top tourist attractions in the United States are Yosemite, in California, and Yellowstone National Park, in Wyoming. Yosemite is home to black bears, while Yellowstone is home to both black and grizzly bears. Every year a few travelers have trouble with bears.

National Park signs warn visitors about bears. Maybe bears also need signs warning them about humans?

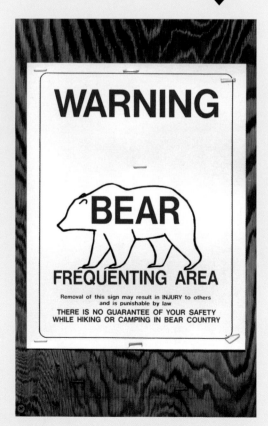

Bearing up

Although the risk of an encounter with a bear is low, it is wise to be wary on travels through these and other parks. More often than not, the traveler is at fault and not the bear! So, just in case you will be traveling in an area where bears live, here are some useful trips:

- Make loud noises if hiking on trails.

- Don't hike after dark.

- Avoid approaching any dead animals, since bears often defend them because they are a source of food.

- If you encounter a bear, don't run. Bears can run faster than Olympic sprinters! If the bear is unaware of you, detour away from the bear. If the bear is aware of you but has not acted aggressively, slowly back away.

- Climbing a tree is sometimes advisable, but not very practical. All North American bears, both black and grizzly, can climb trees.

- Never feed bears. Hang food and anything with strong smells out of the reach of bears, if possible from trees far from the tent! If no trees are available, store your food in airtight or specially designed bear-proof containers.

SAFE OR SORRY?

1) If you got lost in another country, would you:
a) walk to the city center and look for signs to the tourist information office?
b) scream and run up to the nearest passer-by?
c) climb to the top of a church tower for a better view?

2) If your money was stolen when you were far from home, would you:
a) find a police station and report the details?
b) sit in the street and cry?
c) ask everyone in the street if they took your money?

3) If a stranger knocked on your hotel door, would you:
a) use the door security chain and refuse to let them in?
b) shout at them to go away and set off an alarm?
c) welcome them in for a drink and a chat?

4) If one of your friends was missing and you were in an unfamiliar city, would you:
a) call their mobile phone and go to where you agreed to meet in an emergency?
b) run to the police in a panic, shouting "emergency!"?
c) carry on as normal and hope they show up?

5) If a tornado was forecast to hit your vacation resort, would you:
a) ask advice at the hotel and stay calm?
b) scream to everyone to join you lying face-down in a ditch?
c) go swimming to get out of the way?

See page 50 to find out how safe a traveler you are!

Think Green

No book about travel can ignore the effect tourism is having on our planet. People moving from one place to another use a lot of energy, and that means there is always a cost to the environment. Much of the energy we use for transportation leaves pollution behind.

CARBON FOOTPRINT

Many places are trying to reduce the amount of carbon dioxide they release into the atmosphere. So travelers need to think about the impact they might be making with their "carbon footprint." This is the total amount of carbon dioxide we each produce that has an impact on the environment.

Getting it Right

- Do you really need to take that plane? Could you get to your destination using more **eco-friendly** ways of travel? How about exploring areas closer to home?

- Before booking a vacation with a tour operator, travelers should ask whether the company has a "green policy." Cleaner travel sometimes costs more, so if people are serious about saving the planet, they should be prepared to pay a little extra.

- When hiking, always stay on marked trails and stay a safe distance from any animals. Put garbage in garbage cans or take it home. Light campfires only in designated areas, well away from dry grass and trees, making sure the ashes are cold before leaving.

- When diving in the ocean, do not touch coral or stir up sediment, since these actions can damage a reef's fragile **ecosystem**.

- Buy local products whenever possible, instead of goods flown or shipped in from overseas. This will support local people and their economy.

Nearly one billion tourists crisscross the globe every year. Therefore it is more important than ever for travelers to respect the Earth that they want to explore. So when visiting the world's beautiful places, keep this old saying in mind:

> *"Take nothing but photographs, leave nothing but footprints, kill nothing but time."*
>
> *Unknown*

Some airlines are soon hoping to use bio-fuel, which is far cleaner for the environment.

Bon voyage!

By traveling we can learn so much more about the world, others, and ourselves. Traveling should help us all to respect others and become more sensitive to other people's customs, beliefs, and lifestyles. Every traveler has a responsibility to respect the landscape, people, and wildlife they visit, as well as the wider environment. Especially with growing fears that global warming may damage forever the very places we long to visit.

There are sometimes risks, but with care, the whole experience of traveling can be amazing. We all have a part to play—so enjoy thoughtful travel!

GETTING THERE
For page 19

If you mostly answered:
a) You prefer your own company and are quite independent. You travel to get away from the rat-race.

b) You want a cheap vacation to save as much money as you can.

c) You like a bit of luxury, good company, and you don't mind what it costs.

HAVING FUN
For page 39

If you mostly answered:
a) You're so laid-back that you don't bother with much preparation—so anything could happen!

b) You're lively and want to enjoy an active vacation with lots of friends.

c) You take planning seriously but may be a little overcautious at times!

SAFE OR SORRY?
For page 47

If you mostly answered:
a) You remain calm and sensible in a crisis, making you a good traveling companion.

b) You panic easily and do not cope well in a crisis.

c) You haven't taken this book, or its advice, seriously.

20 Things To Remember

1. The number-one rule when packing is "if in doubt, leave it out" to avoid taking too much.

2. A good online currency converter can show the value of most world currencies when you travel abroad.

3. *Never* hitchhike on your travels, even in a group.

4. Ginger or peppermint may help if you suffer from seasickness or general travel sickness.

5. When flying, check flight times and possible delays online before leaving for the airport.

6. When making a hotel reservation by phone or online, keep a record of the confirmation number, the name of the person who took the reservation, and the quoted cost. Keep this in case there is a problem on arrival.

7. For young people needing cheap, reliable accommodation for just a night or two, try an approved youth hostel.

8. When looking for a spot to pitch a tent, avoid windy hilltops and the bottom of hills, where you're at risk of being blown away or flooded.

9. Leave a copy of your travel plans with someone back home so, if you lose anything, help is an email or phone call away.

10. Wherever you are, keep with friends/leaders, don't wander off alone, and always have a mobile phone handy.

11. Don't drink tap water when abroad; don't brush your teeth with it—just in case.

12. Worried about food poisoning and not sure what to eat? Try piping hot pizza—usually safe from bacteria!

13. Always take and use mosquito repellent and sleep under a mosquito net in the tropics.

14. Salty snacks and water or sports drinks should be consumed on any hike lasting longer than 30 minutes.

15. Keep a copy of your hotel's name and phone number on you at all times, in case you get lost.

16. Use a money belt, and don't carry all your cash at once.

17. Avoid being the victim of crime by not looking too flashy or like a typical tourist.

18. When hiking, always stay on marked trails and keep a safe distance from animals. In bear country, be loud so they know to keep away.

19. Buying local products on your travels supports the local economy and is all part of "green travel."

20. Keep in touch with the folks back home— either by regular e-mails or texts.

FURTHER INFORMATION

WEBSITES

http://www.who.int/ith/en
Find out what you need to know about vaccinations before you go!

http://www.greyhound.com
Get ticket and route information for the U.S. and Canada.

http://www.eurolines.com
See how to travel by bus to more than 500 destinations in Europe.

http://www.hihostels.com
Make the most of your hostel experience by knowing where to go.

http://www.abc-of-hiking.com
Information about everything and anything related to hiking and camping.

http://www.hostels.com
This is a mega-database of more than 10,000 hostels to check out.

http://www.lonelyplanet.com
Travel advice and information for just about every place on the planet.

http://www.dk.com
Illustrated travel guides, complete with maps of the best sights to visit.

http://www.weather.com
Weather reports for the U.S. and international destinations.

http://realtravel.com
Get advice from other travelers.

http://www.travel.state.gov
U.S. Department of State provides tips for traveling abroad, document requirements, and information on conditions abroad that may affect travel safety and security.

http://www.pbs.org/americanfieldguide
More than 1,400 video clips providing information on the U.S. outdoors.

http://www.usa.gov/citizen/topics/travel/international.shtml
Links to tourism websites of U.S. states and U.S. territories.

http://www.nps.gov/history/nr/about.htm
A list of 2,400 National Historic Landmarks in the U.S.

BOOKS/GUIDES

Fodor's 1,001 Smart Travel Tips. New York: Fodor's, 2008.

Make the Most of Your Time on Earth: Rough Guide to the World, 1,000 Ultimate Travel Experiences. New York: Rough Guides, 2007.

Rosendo, Joseph. *Where to Go When*. New York: DK Publishing, 2007.

Torkells, Erik. *The Smart Traveler's Passport: 399 Tips from Seasoned Travelers*. Philadelphia: Quirk Books, 2007.

GLOSSARY

acupressure method of applying pressure on specific points of the body to control pain and sickness

allergy abnormal reaction (like sneezing, itching, or rashes) to substances and situations

anti-malarial serving to prevent, control, or cure malaria

dehydration loss of water or body fluids

dormitory room for sleeping, especially for several people

ecosystem system made up of living things interacting with their environment

eco-friendly ecologically acceptable; not harmful or threatening to the environment

embassy office of an ambassador and staff representing a country overseas

etiquette rules governing the proper way to behave

exchange rate rate at which one currency may be converted into another

homesick longing for home and family while away from them

hurricane type of storm featuring violent winds, rain, thunder, and lightning

immune system system that protects the body from foreign substances and disease

jaywalking walking across a street outside of marked crossings or against a signal light

long-haul traveling for eight or more hours

malaria disease passed by the bite of mosquitoes, and marked by attacks of chills and fever

micro-organisms microscopic life or less than microscopic size (such as bacteria)

nationals people who are under the protection of a nation

phobia unreasonable and lasting fear of something

prestigious important in the eyes of many people

sanitation sewage systems and water treatment to promote hygiene and prevent disease

tandem bicycle for two riders

tornado destructive, whirling wind, with a funnel-shaped cloud that moves across the land

tsunami giant ocean wave caused by an earthquake at sea

vaccinations vaccines, usually by injection, that protect against disease

visa document that may be required for someone to enter another country or to stay there for a long period

wind chill temperature felt on exposed skin due to wind speed—colder than the air temperature

YHA Youth Hostel Association

Index